Cries of the Heart

Cries of the Heart
Praying Our Losses

by

Wayne Simsic

Saint Mary's Press
Christian Brothers Publications
Winona, Minnesota

Genuine recycled paper with
10% post-consumer waste.
Printed with soy-based ink.

The publishing team included Carl Koch, FSC, development editor; Mary Duerson Kraemer, copy editor; Alan S. Hanson, production editor and typesetter; inside illustrations by Michael McGrath; cover design by Tom Lowes; cover photo by Wayne Simsic; prepress, printing, and binding by the graphics division of Saint Mary's Press.

The acknowledgments continue on page 81.

Printed in the United States of America

Printing: 9 8 7 6 5 4 3 2 1

Year: 2003 02 01 00 99 98 97 96 95 94

ISBN 0-88489-335-9

May those who sow in tears
reap with songs of joy.
(Psalm 126:5)

CONTENTS

INTRODUCTION

To Those Who Have Experienced a Loss

This book of prayers is for those who are currently grieving and for those who are confronting past losses. These prayers are written to help you face grief issues like forgiveness, shock, depression, and the fear of letting go. They provide words that you may need when your heart is preoccupied with pain.

Death is certainly the most obvious type of loss, but it is not the only kind. We may lose our health, relationships, jobs, fertility, money, self-esteem, youth, reputation, sense of security, a cherished goal, or dreams of the future. Even life transitions that we take for granted, like moving to a new home, involve a painful letting go that cannot easily be dismissed. Letting go of anyone or anything we love hurts. One thing is certain: we will all frequently experience loss in our lifetime.

Each loss is personal and unique. Another person cannot fully enter our pain and understand it. Yet in many ways, all people go through the same process because we are all part of the human community. Thus, we can help each other in our grieving because we journey together.

What Is Grief?

Grief is the painful process of adjusting to a loss. No matter how much inner strength we may have or how strong our faith is, we are destined to grieve. Even though God delivered the people of the Exodus from slavery, they grieved and had to face the hardship of the wilderness before they found the Promised Land. They experienced brokenness before realizing that God traveled with them every step of the way. Grieving is a kind of exodus. We get lost in the desert of our suffering and want to turn back. Nevertheless, the God who journeys with us can lead the way out of the desert to green pastures.

If someone dies, someone whose soul has been linked to our own, the grief can be overwhelming. When a friend and mentor of mine died of cancer, I did not grieve for him at the time. Months later I picked up a book he had written. When I saw his name and recalled how he had helped others through his teaching, the emotions that had been carefully stored in a dark corner of my heart broke free, and I wept. Such a relationship is a gift. Our grief honors this gift and simultaneously guides us to a point of letting go.

Grief is not a hurdle that we can jump over at will or a barrier that we can avoid if we are careful. After his wife's death from cancer, C. S. Lewis recognized the all-encompassing reality of grief: "Her absence is like the sky, spread over everything" (*A Grief Observed*, p. 11). To come to light, healthy grieving leads us through the darkness and transforms us. Whether the loss is great or small, we must grieve it if we are to move on to new life.

Life inevitably brings losses about which we have little choice, but we can choose how we respond to the losses. We can own the changes that the loss has caused in our life, take time to enter our feelings, and ask for help from other people and from God.

Our culture tempts us to ignore grief, to escape through work, drink, sleep, or frenzied activity. However, if we do not grieve, the old hurt and pain will continue to haunt us each time we encounter a new loss.

How Do We Deal with a Loss?

Generally, grieving follows certain movements. We begin grieving by acknowledging or naming our loss. Then, we allow ourselves to feel the pain and express it. Next, healing continues as we realize the blocks to letting go of the grief. Finally, we choose new life.

These stages provide guidelines, but the grieving process cannot be restricted to any neat pattern of behavior. The movements of grieving overlap. One movement may be more difficult than the others and take longer to navigate. We do not all move through the phases in the same way or at the same speed.

One common element to healing our grief is the need for spiritual resources. Like Job, we need to discover our faith again, this time from the perspective of a heart in agony. The wounded heart cries out for help. This cry becomes a spontaneous prayer throughout the day. When our own words fail us, we can turn to the biblical psalms, hymns, favorite poems, or books. Originating in the heart, the psalms echo our own cry of anguish, our own anger, bitterness, doubt, and despair. The psalms ring true because they lament honestly and forcefully. Praying the psalms can allow us to find our voice in times of suffering. Hymns, poems, and passages from books also provide voice for our grief.

The painful process of grieving urges us to rely on God. The Gospels invite us to trust God and surrender to a power greater than ourselves. Even in the bleakest times, God remains near, inviting us gently to hand over our life to infinite love. This love will never abandon us. The journey from sorrow to peace, from anger to harmony cannot be made in isolation. We need God and those people who most sensitively mediate God's love for us.

Using These Prayers

The prayers in the book, though they are broken up into stages, do not have to be used in any particular order. Use them in your prayer as you need them.

At the beginning of each prayer, pause and place yourself in God's loving presence. Let yourself touch feelings of pain, loneliness, despair, love, or hope. Pray slowly. Let the meaning of the words take shape for you. You may want to include other prayers, readings, silent pauses, or dialog with God as you go along. Let these prayers reinforce your heart's ongoing cry to God and provide words when you need them.

Other suggestions:
- Make a commitment to spend at least fifteen minutes a day on the grieving process: praying, walking, performing different rituals, or just remaining silent.
- Practice deep, slow, meditative breathing to pray with greater awareness. Slowly inhale and exhale, repeating a short phrase to yourself like "God be with me" or "Jesus, healer."
- The grief process is exhausting. Take time to rest. In many cases this may be your form of prayer.
- Accept support and care from friends and family and especially from those who have experienced a similar loss.
- Rely on spiritual beliefs, rituals, and meditation practices that you find valuable. By meditation I mean any activity that calms the mind, like jogging, walking, dancing, or concentration on breathing.
- Be a friend to yourself and do not take on unnecessary challenges and responsibilities. They will only drain you and distract your attention from the task of grieving.
- Accept your feelings (guilt, anger, depression) and let them enter your prayer. Bring your

entire self before God just like the psalmists
did.

- Keep a journal or diary. Writing helps you
  acknowledge and honor your thoughts and
  emotions, and thus provides a way to work
  through them. Do not force yourself to write,
  but do so when you feel the need. Writing
  can become a way of praying.
- Laugh. Laughter may be a healing form of
  prayer. Humor allows us to respond more
  humanly to our loss.
- Forgive yourself, and forgive the other person. Put yourself in the presence of God's
  love and let go of any shortcomings, harsh
  words, unexpressed feelings, actions not per-
  formed, mistakes you or the other person
  made. Without forgiveness, we will not be
  open to God's healing love.
- Honor your own experience and the experience of others who grieve.
- Above all, be assured that you will heal. You
  will get better. God is not far away. You only
  have to ask for help, and you will realize that
  love was present all along, waiting for you to
  reach out and embrace it.

Now, in the belief that you can be healed, pray
the familiar and comforting words of Psalm 23.

Yahweh, you are my shepherd;
I shall not want.
In verdant pastures you give me repose.
Beside restful waters you lead me;
you refresh my soul.

You guide me in right paths
for your name's sake.
Even though I walk in the dark valley
I fear no evil;
for you are at my side.

(Vv. 1–4)

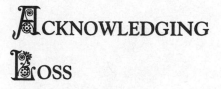CKNOWLEDGING LOSS

To pass through our grief, we must first face the truth that someone or something we love is gone.

But God has said:

"I will
never
leave
you
or
forsake
you."

(Hebrews 13:5)

SHOCK

Opening: O God, I am shattered, my heart lies open and wounded. One moment everything was ordinary, secure. Then suddenly my life was on the edge of an abyss, and I was falling. Time has stopped, and nothing seems important anymore. I don't care to eat. People walk by me as if everything is normal, not realizing that my heart is being torn apart.

Psalm

Yahweh, my God, I call for help all day;
I cry out to you all night.
May my prayer come to you.
Hear my cries for help,
for my soul is troubled.

. . . . . .

I am alone, down among the dead,

. . . .

among those you have forgotten,
those deprived of your care.
You have plunged me to the bottom of the pit,
into its very bottom.

(Psalm 88:1–6)

Reflection

Our first tendency is to escape the shock of grief and get on with our life, but grief will not

18

just disappear. It insists on taking its course and smashing us down like a tidal wave.

We live through the shock, stumbling through life day by day, reading sentences without concen trating, and staring in a daze out windows. Shock serves as the initial line of defense that enables us to carry on under overwhelming sorrow. It is a temporary escape that prepares us for the next stage of grief.

Rather than ignore shock, perhaps we should take time to pour out our feelings in a letter, in a mournful song, or in a lamentation prayer to the person or thing lost.

Hymn

Cry aloud, then, to God,
let your tears flow like a torrent,
day and night;
give yourself no relief,
grant your eyes no rest.

> (Adapted from Lamentations 2:18)

Closing: O God, the loneliness I feel has no language, only a cry. My heart has filled with sorrow. I am beyond help. Day and night I raise my voice to you, hoping for an answer. Hear my plea, O God, and do not abandon me. The wound in my heart will not heal.

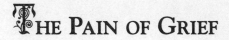HE PAIN OF GRIEF

Opening: Merciful God, I am confused, lonely, and sad. I do not feel like talking with people. Emotions drain my strength, leaving me numb and hopeless. Tears well up at unexpected times. What am I to do, O God? I have no control. Give me the strength to bear these bitter tears.

Psalm

Like the deer that yearns
for running streams,
so my soul is yearning
for you, my God.
My tears have become my food night and day,
and I hear it said all day long:
"Where is your God?"
Why are you so sad, my soul?
Why sigh within me?
Hope in God.

(Psalm 42:1,3,5)

Reflection

Grief rushes in, abates for a time, then rushes in again. The immense pain takes away words. We receive news that a friend has died, that we have a chronic illness, that we have lost our job, or that we have sustained some other loss.

Dreadful images storm our imagination. Yet we cannot dismiss the pain. Any attempt to do so only intensifies the anguish.

We carry the weight of grief from month to month, until we are finally willing to let go. None of this is controlled. Feelings of denial, anger, and the harsh reality of pain rule our life. Jesus wept during his prayer at Gethsemane and said to his followers, "My soul is sorrowful to the point of death" (adapted from Matthew 26:38). In our suffering, we repeat the same words and try to find in them not weakness but transformation.

Hymn

I am the one familiar with misery
under the rod of God's anger;
I am the one God has forced to walk
in darkness, and without any light.
God holds up a hand against me alone,
again and again, all day long.
        (Adapted from Lamentations 3:1–3)

Closing: Give me the strength, merciful God, to pass through my pain, and let it transform my soul. Teach me to express my grief honestly, to cry, and to weather the onslaught of emotions while trusting in you.

FEELING HELPLESS
AND VULNERABLE

Opening: This loss has stripped me, faithful
God, and made me feel disoriented, helpless,
and alone. I am overwhelmed and want to close
the door and hide.

Psalm

Create a pure heart in me, O my God;
renew me with a steadfast spirit.
My sacrifice is this broken spirit.
You will not disdain a contrite and humbled
   heart.

(Psalm 51:10,17)

Reflection

The reality of our loss, as we become more
aware of it, strips away our old ways of seeing,
exposes illusions toward ourselves, the world,
and God. It compels us to search our heart.

And yet, strangely, it is in this helplessness
that we come upon the beginning of joy. We
discover that as long as we stay still the pain is
not so bad and there is even a certain peace, a
certain richness, a certain strength, a certain
companionship that makes itself present to us
when we are beaten down and lie flat with our

mouths in the dust, hoping for hope. (Thomas Merton, *New Seeds of Contemplation*, p. 263)

Hymn

We wake up in a room not our own,
carry on with no sense of life,
bearing the weight of our helplessness—
not out of strength,
not out of hope,
but because habits remain unchanged
and we need to push on.
God help us.

Closing: Faithful God, create a new heart within this chaos; let me find a way through brokenness and wounds. Bring me out of hiding and into the light. Let me understand that as surely as I am emptied, I will someday be filled with joy and new life.

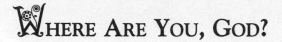WHERE ARE YOU, GOD?

Opening: It is winter in my heart, God, and
you do not respond to my utter depression and
isolation. You promise no relief. You do not
break the silence and turn back this bitter wind
that chills me to the bone.

Psalm

My God, my God, why have you deserted me?
Far from my prayer, from the words I cry?
I call all day, my God, but you never answer;
all night long I call and cannot rest.
My throat is drier than baked clay
and my tongue sticks to my mouth.

(Psalm 22:1–2,15)

Reflection

But go to Him when your need is desperate,
when all other help is vain, and what do you
find? A door slammed in your face, and a sound
of bolting and double bolting on the inside.
After that, silence. You may as well turn away.
The longer you wait, the more emphatic the
silence will become. . . . What can this mean?
Why is He so present a commander in our time
of prosperity and so very absent a help in time
of trouble? (C. S. Lewis, *A Grief Observed*,
pp. 4–5)

Hymn

I saw no anger
in God,
neither for a short time
nor for long.
For, as I see it,
if God could be angry
even for a second
we would lose
life, place and being.
Even though we feel angry,
we are still embraced
by God's gentleness, care, and compassion.

(Adapted from Julian of Norwich,
Showings, p. 264)

Closing: If only I could see a sign of hope,
God, some signal to continue the journey. Your
voice is at best barely audible. Fill the cold
spaces of my heart with the warm announce-
ment of your healing love.

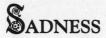ADNESS

Opening: Gracious God, give me strength to bear this loss in the days ahead. My heart breaks and sadness overwhelms me.

Psalm

Let your tears flow like a river day and night,
day and night;
do not rest,
let yourself weep.

Cry out at night,
in the early hours of darkness;
pour your heart out like water
before God.

> (Adapted from Lamentations 2:18,19)

Reflection

After Lazarus died Jesus wept. Bystanders who witnessed this realized how much Jesus loved his friend.

The pain of a loss rises up from the depths of the heart and brings us to tears. It cannot be explained, only endured. People may try to console us with the promise that time will heal. But we do not want to lose our grief because it is bound up with our love. When grief begins to fill our heart, any attempt to divert it threatens the significance of our response.

Hymn

My dear friend,
I am glad
you have come
to me
in all your sadness.
I have always
been with you,
and now
you see my love,
and we are one,
in joy.

(Adapted from Julian of Norwich,
Showings, p. 246)

Closing:
May those who sow in tears
reap with songs of joy!
Those that go forth weeping,
carrying the seed for sowing,
shall come home with shouts of joy.

(Psalm 126:5–6)

LEARNING TO TRUST

Opening: God of compassion, teach me to
trust in you. I have discovered I can no longer
control every situation. Help me believe that
you have made a home in my heart and will
work in my life in your own time. Teach me to
rest in you untroubled as I wait for your will.

Psalm

Like the deer that yearns
for running streams,
so my soul is yearning
for you, my God.
Why are you so sad, my soul?
Why sigh within me?
Hope in God;
for I will yet praise my savior and my God.

(Psalm 42:1,5)

Reflection

The test comes when everything that is dear to
us slips away—our home and those we love, our
body and its many ways of living, our mind and
its caring thoughts—and there is absolutely
nothing left to hold on to. It is then that one
must have the faith to surrender to a loving
Lord, to believe that he will not allow us to fall
into a cruel and bottomless canyon, but will

bring us to the safe home which he has prepared
for us. (Henri J. M. Nouwen, *In Memoriam*,
pp. 30–31)

Hymn

And though I suffer darknesses
In this mortal life,
That is not so hard a thing;
For though I have no light
I have the light of heaven.
For the blinder love is
The more it gives such life,
Holding the soul surrendered,
Living without light, in darkness.
> (Saint John of the Cross, "Commentary
> Applied to Spiritual Things,"
> *The Collected Works*, p. 735)

Closing: God of compassion, the darkness is so
great it engulfs me entirely. But my intent is to
faithfully trust in you. Trust is not easy, but
even the possibility of trust becomes my guide.
Show me your compassion and grace, and let
me never doubt that you will help me.

Part 2

Feeling Pain

The only way to heal pain is to feel it.

My soul
is exceedingly
sorrowful,
even to
death.

(Adapted from Matthew 26:38)

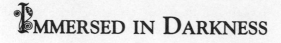MMERSED IN DARKNESS

Opening: God, our hope, I enter the dark womb of grief and cannot escape. Let me find hope in this cavern and beginnings in this dark place. Give me the courage to take a leap of faith, to die with my loss so that I can live.

Psalm

O God, why do you reject me?
Why do you hide your face from me?
I am afflicted and have suffered since my youth;
I bore your fury; now I almost despair.
Your anger overwhelmed me;
you shattered me with your terrors,
which, like a flood, engulfed me all day long—
all together closing in on me.
You have turned my friends and neighbors
    against me;
now darkness is my only friend.

(Psalm 88:14–18)

Reflection

There is wisdom in knowing that we must sometimes experience the darkness before we learn to treasure the light. Often in the loneliness of our suffering, we first realize the grace of a new life.

Faith lights the darkness even if it seems filled with death. Even with our shaken belief, we can hope for tomorrow, affirm freedom, wait for peace, and defy the forces of selfishness, fear, and cowardice. We can also pray like the father of the possessed boy in the Gospel story: "I have faith. Help my lack of faith!" (adapted from Mark 9:25).

Hymn

I said to my soul, be still, and let the dark come upon you
Which shall be the darkness of God. As, in a theatre,
The lights are extinguished, for the scene to be changed
With a hollow rumble of wings, with a movement of darkness on darkness.

(T. S. Eliot, *Four Quartets*, p. 27)

Closing: You force me, God our hope, to uncover hidden strengths during a time of insecurity and powerlessness. You draw me into unknown regions, along hidden paths, so that suffering can transform me in life-giving ways.

Loss Influences All We See

Opening: God, why did you break my secure shell and throw me into a strange, threatening world? My passion for life deserts me, dreams disappear, and I walk in the shadows.

Psalm

I am like a pelican living in the wilderness,
or a screech owl haunting the ruins.
I lie awake moaning
like some lonely bird on the rooftops.
The bread I eat has become like ashes;
what I drink is mixed with my tears.
Yahweh, you will answer the prayer of the
  helpless
and will not laugh at their plea.

(Psalm 102:6–7,9,17)

Reflection

In our grief, loss spreads over our life like a dark cloud influencing all that we see. No activity escapes its shadow.

We think about our loss almost all the time. It is never far from the surface of our mind when we eat, walk, fall asleep.

Daily routine no longer offers safe harbor from sadness, and our sanity seems threatened

by images from the past. The specter of loss
hovers over us, sapping our energy, draining our
desire.

Hymn

It seemed to me
that my sorrow
exceeded death itself. . . .

Of all the pain
that leads to freedom
this is the greatest—
to see someone we love
suffer.

How could any pain be greater
than to see the person
who is all my life,
all my happiness,
and all my joy
suffer?

(Adapted from Julian of Norwich,
Showings, p. 209)

Closing: Others notice my eyes glisten with
tears, God, when I am trying to act normal. I
remain powerless in the face of this loss. Do not
abandon me to the darkness. Help me go on
though I have lost my way.

CRYING OUT TO GOD

Opening: Weary, worn out in body and spirit, I cry out to you, my God. My heart pours out to your compassionate presence. Release me from this suffering.

Psalm

O God, rescue me!
The waters are up to my chin.
I am wallowing in quicksand
with no foothold for safety.
I have slipped into deep water;
the waves pound over me.
I am exhausted from calling;
my throat is parched.

(Psalm 69:1–3)

Reflection

The world goes about its business as if our loss did not matter. Others cannot imagine our abandonment. There is no one to turn to. The ache of our heart reminds us how much human life is inextricably bound up with pain. Easter seems absurd, the Resurrection impossible. Life leads to tears; love brings sorrow. We cry out. Only God can help.

Hymn

There is no end of it, the voiceless wailing,
No end to the withering of withered flowers,
To the movement of pain that is painless and
    motionless,
To the drift of the sea and the drifting wreckage,
The bone's prayer to Death its God. Only the
    hardly, barely prayable
Prayer of the one Annunciation.

(T. S. Eliot, Four Quartets, p. 38)

Closing: The voiceless cry of my sorrow creeps up my spine and threatens to drown me, my God. Protect me; strengthen me with your love; keep me from despair. Give me confidence in your will so that I can once again experience the light and warmth of life.

EXPRESSING FEELINGS

Opening: God of truth, I know that I must learn to uncover my grief and express it. Give me the strength to face my emotions honestly, to weep, to release my grief, so that I can be healed. Tears give me hope that the pain can be washed away.

Psalm

You are my God, so be merciful to me.
I call to you all day long.
Make your servant glad,
because I lift my soul to you.
Listen to my prayer;
hear my cry for help.
I call to you in times of trouble,
for you answer my prayer.
Teach me your way, Yahweh,
and I will obey you faithfully.

(Psalm 86:3–4,6–7,11)

Reflection

Mourning the death of his mother, Monica, Saint Augustine reflected:

I took comfort in weeping in your sight over her and for her, over myself and for myself. I gave way to the tears that I had held back, so that they poured forth as much as they wished.

I spread them beneath my heart, and it rested upon them, for at my heart were placed your ears, not the ears of a mere man, who would interpret with scorn my weeping. (*The Confessions of St. Augustine*, p. 226)

Hymn

Crushed and broken,
my spirit overwhelmed,
I am unable to find the right path.
I move slowly, one foot in front of the
    other . . .
but this is enough.
I forge a new way
by remaining faithful to small rituals,
acting out my feelings
with long walks,
crying out,
listening to sad songs,
but
not giving up,
continuing forward
toward healing and new life.

Closing: Did you know, God of truth, how much I long to express the hurt I hide within? I know nothing can change this devastating loss in my life, but open the door of my heart and help me heal the pain.

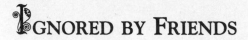GNORED BY FRIENDS

Opening: Ever present God, I feel abandoned. Even an awkward glance from a friend has the effect of a rejection. Becoming tired of my mourning, they seem to shun me in my grief. How long will I suffer this grief in my heart?

Psalm

Take pity on me, Yahweh;
I am in trouble now.
Sorrow consumes my eyes,
my throat, my inmost parts.
To every one of my oppressors
I am contemptible;
loathsome to my neighbors,
and to my friends a thing of fear.
Those who see me in the street hurry past me;
I am forgotten, as good as dead in their hearts,
something discarded.

(Psalm 31:9,11–12)

Reflection

Feelings of isolation are overwhelming during the stage of grief that involves feeling the pain. Some friends grow weary of our sorrow and turn away. Others offer advice that comes down to, "Snap out of it." Other people pretend not to see us and act as if our loss does not exist.

We are tempted to hide away in silence, to muffle our complaints. But wisdom teaches us to confront our feelings of alienation and to begin reinvesting our love in other people who are hurting as well. As we look at others through the window of our grief, we will find ourselves ministering with empathy and compassion. No matter what, we need the cleansing of a free expression of our anguish.

Hymn

No man is an island, entire of itself;
every man is a piece of the continent,
a part of the main. . . .
Any man's death diminishes me
because I am involved in mankind,
and therefore never send to know
for whom the bell tolls;
it tolls for thee.

(John Donne, "Meditation XVII")

Closing: Answer me, ever present God. Turn toward me, and embrace me with love. Rescue me when all my support fails. "Insults have broken my heart. / I am helpless. / I looked for sympathy, but there was none" (Psalm 69:20).

EMOTIONAL TURMOIL

Opening: I am not resigned to this loss, God of mercy. My feelings of quick and passionate anger, guilt, despair, and hope erupt in my heart, causing chaos and confusion. I am in the grasp of an anguish that controls me. Protect me so that I do not get totally lost in my feelings.

Psalm

My only food is sighs,
and my groans pour out like water.
Whatever I fear comes true,
whatever I dread befalls me.
For me, there is no calm, no peace;
my torments banish rest.

(Adapted from Job 3:24–26)

Reflection

When we turned into the road leading to our house, I suddenly felt a deep, inner sadness. Tears came to my eyes and I did not dare to look at my father. We both understood. She would not be home. She would not open the door and embrace us. She would not ask how the day had been. . . . I felt an anxious tension when my father drove into the garage and we walked up to the door. Upon entering the house it was suddenly clear to us: it had become an empty house. (Henri J. M. Nouwen, *In Memoriam*, p. 48)

Hymn

Ah my dear angry Lord,
Since thou dost love, yet strike;
Cast down, yet help afford;
Sure I will do the like.

I will complain, yet praise;
I will bewail, approve:
And all my sour-sweet days
I will lament, and love.
(George Herbert, "Bitter-Sweet")

Closing: Come near, God of mercy, and calm my inner struggle. What emotion is worth pursuing? Release me from the bonds of anger, sadness, and confusion. Let me address one feeling at a time so that I can see more clearly.

Words Offer No Comfort

Opening: God of my life, the reality of my loss makes all language seem artificial and inadequate. Words are dwarfed by my feelings. Let me find some meaning in this inexpressible, unreasonable silence.

Psalm

I am utterly spent and crushed;
I groan because of the anguish of my heart.
Yahweh, all my longing is known to you;
my sighing is not hidden from you.
My heart throbs and my strength fails me;
the light of my eyes has gone from me.
My friends and companions stand aloof from
    my plague,
and my neighbors stand afar off.

(Psalm 38:8–11)

Reflection

The winter of grief offers no words to describe the sorrow. The mourning heart breaks in the cold silence. Tears congeal and the lethargic soul retreats to a secret room, struck dumb with sorrow.

We should be still and let the silence befriend us. We may hear what we have refused to listen to, and find words that previously remained un-said. In the cavern of silent emptiness, we may begin to realize clearly that we are finite and that no words will release us from this condition.

Hymn

A grief without a pang, void, dark, and drear,
    A stifled, drowsy, unimpassioned grief,
    Which finds no natural outlet, no relief,
In word, or sigh, or tear—

        (Samuel Taylor Coleridge, "Dejection")

Closing: I desperately search for answers in this awesome stillness, God of my life. Where can I find direction except from you? To you I look for support. "God is good to those who wait in trust, to the soul that searches for divine relief. Waiting patiently for God to save will be rewarded" (adapted from Lamentations 3:25–26).

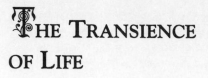

The Transience of Life

Opening: Wise God, no words describe this sense that my life is quickly ending. Give me the strength to fight the pull of hopelessness. Help me grow to accept my mortality.

Psalm

"Yahweh, you have shown me my end.
How short is the length of my days!
Now I know how fleeting my life is.
You have given me a short span of days;
my life is as nothing in your sight.
A mere breath is human life,
a mere shadow passing by;
a mere breath, the riches they hoard,
not knowing who will have them."

(Psalm 39:4–6)

Reflection

After a painful loss, we may awaken abruptly in the middle of the night feeling the quick passage of time. The sound of a branch clicking against the roof, the rhythm of the clock, the drip in the bathroom sink mark each escaping moment.

Years have faded into whispers barely audible in the thick night silence. We know that we will rise in the morning barely remembering these twilight visions. Yet we might feel the need to stop during the day, glance through a window, and remind ourselves to relish the mystery of our life.

Hymn

Gather ye rosebuds while ye may,
    Old Time is still a-flying;
And the same flower that smiles today
    Tomorrow will be dying.

The glorious lamp of heaven, the sun,
    The higher he's a-getting,
The sooner will his race be run,
    And nearer he's to setting.

             (Robert Herrick,
     "To the Virgins to Make Much of Time")

Closing: Awareness of my fragility, wise God, threatens to deaden my spirit and take the effort out of my work. Teach me to enjoy the beauty of each day and celebrate life's sacred moments: "Make us realize the shortness of life / that we may gain wisdom of heart" (Psalm 90:12).

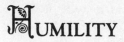UMILITY

Opening: Saving God, you have shaken my secure ground. I never thought I could lose control. Will I drown in this dark abyss? Will you save me? I can no longer save myself. Help me!

Psalm

Yahweh, my heart has no false pride;
my eyes do not look too high.
I am not concerned with great affairs
or things far above me.
It is enough for me to keep my soul still and
   quiet
like a child in its mother's arms.

(Psalm 131:1–2)

Reflection

God draws close to those whose spirit is crushed and whose courage is broken (adapted from Psalm 34:18). We lose control, fall to our knees, but our humiliation is not a punishment. It is a call to wake up.

When our loss teaches us that we cannot control life, a surprising thing happens: we are able to hear God's answer to our suffering. God speaks, and we are invited to respond with our entire being. Stripped of the illusion of our control, we are graced with an awareness of what is truly important.

Hymn

Weak and fearful, I ask,
where is my true strength?
Drowning in dark water,
where is my rescuer?
Crushed by loss,
where is my savior?
My heart aches,
my efforts fail.
Come near, O God,
strengthen, rescue, save me.
Praise to you, O Holy One!

Closing: Saving God, when all else fails I turn to you. You are the horizon beyond all other horizons, the final net that catches me. Teach me the path of true humility so that I can learn to share in your strength and love.

PART 3

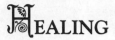

HEALING

If we continue to struggle through the
painful times, even though progress seems
minimal, we uncover an inner strength
and realize what is truly important in life.

And we heal.
These
sufferings
bring
patience.

(Romans 5:7)

Putting Life
Back in Order

Opening: Merciful God, facing my loss made me discover what is really important in my life and has changed me. Gaining a new perspective has lessened the pain and deepened the sadness. But I am ready to move forward.

Psalm

All this has happened to us, but we do not
     forget you
and have not betrayed your covenant;
we have not gone back on our purpose,
nor have our feet strayed from your path.

(Psalm 44:17–18)

Reflection

It is time to accept God's promise and embrace the new, though maybe unwelcome, changes in our life. We need to return to work, establish manageable goals, rededicate ourselves to the routine tasks of daily living. Life is not over—we know this. Decisions need to be made so that we can now move on.

  Returning to life again and coping with new situations challenge our resources. We might be more comfortable with our grief. Our loss is special, and most other people probably do not understand how great it is. Yet we know that we must allow normalcy to return and remember the blessings in our life.

Hymn

Sadness is my garden
where cold blossoms grow,
yet winter passes into spring.
For months now,
I have lived with weeping,
bare thickets and long evenings.
But someone told me
that at the edge of the woods
she saw white flowers growing.
I want to go there
and touch a place in my heart
where dreams can refresh
and days grow green with promise.

Closing: Merciful God, I am emerging from the darkness—enough to see the need for transformation and to venture into a new, unpredictable world. No one leaves behind the darkness without suffering and pain. Give me the strength to believe in my life again. Give me confidence and hope. Today is the time for healing.

LEARNING PATIENCE

Opening: God of love, teach me patience. Let me wait to hear your counsel. I was in a hurry to have the pain taken away, to have you fulfill my plans. But now I wait, yearning for light to dispel the darkness. I wait to respond to your wisdom that always leads to wholeness.

Psalm

Let none that wait for you be put to shame;
let them be ashamed who heedlessly break
    faith.
Make me know your ways, Yahweh;
teach me your paths.
Lead me in your truth and teach me,
for you are the God of my salvation;
for you I wait all the day long.

(Psalm 25:3–5)

Reflection

We are not the same after the experience of loss. Grief has provided us with an opportunity to discover our deepest character and to reconsider what is most important in our life.

Grieving is an advent in our life, a time of waiting, a time of yearning for light. We long for a place of inner peace, a secure home within. We no longer want to be strangers to ourselves and to others. Guide us home, God of light.

Hymn

I said to my soul, be still, and wait without hope
For hope would be hope for the wrong thing;
   wait without love
For love would be love of the wrong thing;
   there is yet faith
But the faith and the love and the hope are all
   in the waiting.
Wait without thought, for you are not ready for
   thought:
So the darkness shall be the light, and the
   stillness the dancing.

               (T. S. Eliot, *Four Quartets*, p. 28)

Closing: God of love, lead me out of lonely exile and let me glimpse the homeland. You are the God of all those who wander in darkness. You are the home that my soul cries out for. Grant me the strength and patience to meet the days to come in the joyful expectation of a new life with those I love.

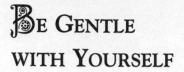 BE GENTLE
WITH YOURSELF

Opening: Holy Friend, it is time to rest more deeply in your care. I need to lie fallow like a plot of land left unseeded so that my heart can once again bear riches. Show me how to be kind to myself and not to worry.

Psalm

Yahweh, you are my shepherd;
I shall not want.
In verdant pastures you give me repose.
Beside restful waters you lead me;
you refresh my soul.
Even though I walk in the dark valley
I fear no evil;
for you are at my side.
Only goodness and kindness follow me
all the days of my life;
and I shall dwell in your house
for years to come.

(Psalm 23:1–3,4,6)

Reflection

"You have survived the winter because you are, and were, and always will be very much loved," said the sun. "For that small place deep within you that remained unfrozen and open to mystery, that is where I have made my dwelling. And long, long before you felt my warmth surrounding you, you were being freed and formed from within in ways so deep and profound that you could not possibly know what was happening." (Mary Fahy, *The Tree That Survived the Winter*)

Hymn

And God said . . .
"Does a woman forget the baby
at her breast,
or fail to cherish her own child?
Yet even if some do forget,
I will never forget you.
You are etched in the palm of my hand.
In your heart you will wonder,
Who has given me these gifts?
I was empty and barren,
who nourished me?
When I was all alone
who stayed with me?"
And God said . . .
"Those who hope in me will never be
    abandoned."

(Adapted from Isaiah 49:15,21)

Closing: Holy Friend, I remember a time when my heart became frozen winter soil, unable to bear any growth. Now I open myself to receive your nourishing rain and warming sun. Thank you for nurturing me and giving me the opportunity to flourish.

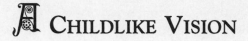 CHILDLIKE VISION

Opening: Holy Light, grief has given me some
clarity of vision. I see my life differently, with
more depth and compassion. Grant me the wisdom to stand before the mystery of all life, free
in spirit like a child.

Psalm

One thing have I asked of you, Yahweh,
this I seek:
to dwell in your house
all the days of my life,
to behold your beauty
and to contemplate on your Temple.
I believe that I shall see the goodness of
    Yahweh
in the land of the living!

(Psalm 27:4,13)

Reflection

Even in the midst of grief and loss, we might
try to depend on rational thinking and seek to
control our life. Further along the journey of
recovery from loss, we are less likely to attempt
to make sense out of everything. We learn the
hard lesson that no explanation truly satisfies.

With a fresh sense of our dependence on
God, we might start to feel like children again,

aware of the small mysteries around us. We do not want to lose touch with the giftedness of our life, and so we might imagine ourselves as children in Jesus' loving embrace: "'Let the little children come to me; do not stop them; for it is to such as these that the kingdom of God belongs'" (Mark 10:14).

Hymn

Once you have
the joy of a child,
it lasts forever
like a dream,
always alive
though buried in adult days
under hurt, losses, and insecurity;
but it rises again,
an island of light
resurrected
in a dark ocean,
when you are struck down
with the weight of grief
and your eyes are opened.
I am eight again.

Closing: May I continue to wonder, God of light, and never stifle my childlike awe at your gifts. After being shocked by pain, I want to be open to mystery in a new, unexpected way. Grace me with ears to hear the song and eyes to see the light of the universe. You invite me to this cosmic dance.

THE FEAR OF LETTING GO

Opening: God of power, give me the strength to make decisions and gently let go of the part of me that holds on to the grief. The time has come to release the pain. Life is not over. Though it will never be the same, it can once again be full.

Psalm

For you, O God, have tested us;
you have tried us as silver is tried.
You brought us into the net,
laying a heavy burden on our backs.

. . . .

We went through fire and through water;
you brought us forth to a spacious place.
I will come into your house with burnt offerings;
I will fulfill the vows
that my lips uttered
and my mouth promised when I was in trouble.

(Psalm 66:10–14)

Reflection

We fear letting go, yet life is a continual process of letting go. Each choice we make entails the loss of other possibilities. We let go of dreams, youth, health, friends, loved ones, and eventually our own life.

Letting go of grief can be the greatest challenge as we mourn. Grief can become a substitute for whomever or whatever we lost. Letting go and feeling better can be perceived as the betrayal of a memory of the loss. Grieving beyond our time, however, threatens our own aliveness.

Letting go hastens our transformation. By surrendering our loss with faith and hope, our exhausted heart can choose new life.

Hymn

I am not ready to die,
But I am learning to trust death
As I have trusted life.
I am moving
Toward a new freedom
Born of detachment,
And a sweeter grace—
Learning to let go.
(May Sarton, "Gestalt at Sixty," Selected Poems, p. 85)

Closing: God of power, letting go challenges me to trust you when the sky is still mostly dark. May Jesus, who lost everything but was transformed with Easter life, remind me of your abiding love for me.

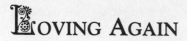OVING AGAIN

Opening: God of love, you shelter me in your embrace. In the face of sadness and despair, you place invitations to love again in my path. In my heart I realize that even when my feelings were most intense and the abyss most threatening, a Yes to life was rising in my soul.

Psalm

If Yahweh had not helped me,
I would have gone quickly to a silent grave.
I said, "I am falling";
but Yahweh, your faithful love supported me.
When I am anxious and worried,
you comfort me and make me glad.

(Psalm 94:17–19)

Reflection

While grieving, we think that we will never love again. The pain of our broken heart can tempt us to desire a heart of stone, a heart invulnerable to the suffering of loss.

Yet God, like a compassionate parent, watches over us, waiting with us, surrounding us with faithful love. God's love does not take away our pain, but God, our faithful companion, will always remain with us in spite of any loss. Gradually, as we heal, we cherish love more dearly and try to live each day as if it were our last.

Hymn

"Come then, my love,
my lovely one, come.
For see, winter is past,
the rains are over and gone.
The flowers appear on the earth.
The season of glad songs has come.
Come then, my love,
my lovely one, come.
show me your face,
let me hear your voice."

(Adapted from Song of Songs 2:10–14)

Closing: God of love, how good it is to feel your gentle presence and life-giving energy. Thank you for creating me in the image of love and watching over me with tenderness and compassion. You are "close to the brokenhearted / and . . . those whose spirit is crushed" (Psalm 34:18).

PART 4

NEW LIFE

Loss changes our vision of life; it can give birth to deeper self-awareness and open our heart to greater love for other people and for God.
You should
carry
each other's
troubles.

(Adapted from Galatians 6:2)

DELIVERED FROM DARKNESS

Opening: Looking at the stars in the night sky, I am reminded that your deliverance, faithful God, is always near, always in the process of coming to fulfillment. The mystery of light on the horizon grows and guides me through these times of trouble.

Psalm

Some sat in gloom and darkness,
prisoners suffering in chains.
Then they cried to Yahweh in their anguish,
and Yahweh rescued them from their distress,
releasing them from gloom and darkness,
shattering their chains.

(Psalm 107:10,13–14)

Reflection

In a last violent protest against the hopelessness of imminent death, I sensed my spirit piercing through the enveloping gloom. I felt it transcend that hopeless, meaningless world, and from somewhere I heard a victorious "Yes" in answer to my question of the existence of an ultimate purpose. At that moment a light was lit in a distant farmhouse, which stood on the horizon as if painted there, in the midst of the miserable grey of a dawning morning. (Viktor E. Frankl, *Man's Search for Meaning*, p. 60)

Hymn

Then I saw a new heaven and a new earth.
I saw the holy city, the new Jerusalem,
coming down out of heaven from God,
prepared as a bride dressed for her husband.
"Look, here God lives among human beings.
God will wipe away all the tears from their
    eyes;
there will be no more death,
and no more mourning and sadness or pain."
The world of the past has gone.
The city did not need the sun or the moon for
    light,
since it was lit by the radiant glory of God.
            (Adapted from Revelation 21:1–4,23)

Closing: Faithful God, I am not troubled by the night. Winter turns to spring. Resurrection swallows up death. I do not worry about the city of today, but yearn for your Reign.

HOPE

Opening: I hope in you, Holy One, although at times there seemed to be no reason for hope. In loneliness and suffering, I unlocked the door where hope hides and quietly embraced your promises. I sing songs to you because you have offered me hope when despair stalked and threatened me.

Psalm

For you alone are my hope.
Yahweh, I have trusted you since my youth;
I have leaned on you since I was born.
You have been my strength from my mother's
    womb
and my constant hope.
You have made me feel misery and hardship,
but you will give me life again.
I promise I will praise you on the lyre
for your faithfulness, O my God.

                (Psalm 71:5–6,20,22)

Reflection

Nothing, not even death, separates a person who hopes from God. So strong is hope that some hold on to it even at the center of chaos and imminent death. Sometimes when we are overcome with hopelessness, we discover an unexpected light deep inside, beyond the conscious mind. We feel there is an answer, if we only have enough patience to wait. Our own plans fail us, so we live on hope, believing as Paul did that "nothing already in existence and nothing still to come . . . will be able to come between us and the love of God, known to us in Christ Jesus" (adapted from Romans 8:39).

Hymn

> Grief melts away
> Like snow in May,
> As if there were no such cold thing.
>
> Who would have thought my shrivelled
>   heart
> Could have recovered greenness? It was gone
>   quite underground; as flowers depart
> To see their mother-root, when they have
>   blown;
>   Where they together
>   All the hard weather,
> Dead to the world, keep house unknown.
>   (George Herbert, "The Flower")

Closing: Let me breathe the air of hope, Holy One. Even though I question everything and sometimes let my expectations get in the way, let me never lose hope. Because my suffering has made me vulnerable, I embrace hope more than ever. Fill me with joy and peace through the power of your Spirit.

Sensitive to the Mystery of Life

Opening: God of compassion, I am no longer looking for an explanation for this loss and have become aware of the horizons beyond my limited mind. Keep me open to the awesome mystery that surrounds my life.

Psalm

Yahweh, you search me and know me.
You know if I am standing or sitting.
You perceive my thoughts from far away.
Whether I walk or lie down, you are watching;
you are familiar with all my ways.
You created my inmost being
and knit me together in my mother's womb.
For all these mysteries—
for the wonder of myself,
for the wonder of your works—
I thank you.

(Psalm 139:1–3; 13–14)

Reflection

No loss is so great that it eliminates the fact that our lives are mystery and that experience and thought, emotion and free will, love and reason will prevail in time.

Things that go wrong or the onslaught of suffering from a loss do not threaten us as much as forgetting the potential of what life can become. The usual boundaries around the self collapse under the weight of a loss, and once again we stand in wonder at one fact: I exist. God invites us to say Yes to life.

Hymn

Yes, certainly God shows us marvels
  and does great deeds that we cannot
  understand.
When [God] says to snow, "Fall on the earth!"
  to the showers, "Now rain hard!"
[God] brings all human activity to a standstill,
  for everyone to acknowledge [God's] work.

Listen to this, Job, without flinching
  and reflect on the marvellous works of God.
                                    (Job 37:5–7,14)

Closing: God of compassion, encountering mystery humbles and frees me at the same time. Let me never take for granted the force of love, the power of tenderness, the warmth of touch, the presence of another, the revelation of suffering. Make my life an empty vessel waiting to be filled; open my hands so that I am always ready to receive.

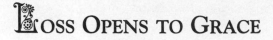LOSS OPENS TO GRACE

Opening: Gracious God, you blessed me with the opportunity to experience new life rising out of the abyss of grief. Give me the strength to bear this process of spiritual death and rebirth, and let me gain wisdom from it.

Psalm

I cried to you for help, my God,
and you healed me.
You brought me back from the world of the
dead.
I was with those who go down to the depths
below,
but you restored my life.
There may be tears during the night,
but joy comes in the morning.

(Psalm 30:2–3,5)

Reflection

We cry ourselves to sleep at night, but wake up to sunrise and grace in the morning. Through loss we experience a spiritual death while still alive. This process seems cruel, but Jesus said it was necessary: the old self needs to die so that a new person can come to life. Good Friday eventually culminates in Easter.

Grieving offers us an opportunity for a new vision. Our loss may diminish our tolerance for old values. Old pleasures may no longer satisfy. Instead we might find unexpected joy in ordinary gestures of love and previously unnoticed expressions of beauty. We can grow increasingly grateful for the goodness without and within and believe that we are truly precious in God's eyes.

Hymn

Rise heart; thy Lord is risen. Sing his praise
    Without delays,
Who takes thee by the hand, that thou likewise
    With him mayst rise.

                (George Herbert, "Easter")

Closing: Gracious God, your ways are mystery. Let me see my grief as a divine gift that offers me a new appreciation for my life and for what is truly important. Keep me awake so that I never take my life for granted and lose the ability to cherish all that I am given.

RECLAIMING JOY AND A SENSE OF HUMOR

Opening: Holy Friend, let me laugh and find joy even while I suffer so that I can find inner peace and put my loss in perspective. Let me praise you and proclaim your goodness.

Psalm

You have changed my sadness into a joyful
    dance;
you have taken off my clothes of mourning
and given me garments of joy.
So I will not be silent;
I will sing praise to you.
Yahweh, you are my God;
I will give thanks to you forever.

(Psalm 30:11–12)

Reflection

If we have faith that God is already present in the world guiding us toward salvation, laughing and crying with us, then we can discover joy even in profoundest grief.

Our recovery from grief may begin with a half-smile at a witty remark. With grace, we may soon laugh at life's many ironies. The gift of humor provides an antidote to unremitting seriousness.

God truly cares for us. We can let go of our efforts to control the universe. The Creator wants us fully alive, fully joyous.

Hymn

Yahweh, your God, is in your midst,
renewing you with love;
dancing with shouts of joy for you
as on a day of festival.

> (Adapted from Zephaniah 3:17–18)

Closing: Holy Friend, join my heart with your joyful song. Set me free from anxieties that only isolate me, fears that stifle my song, and emptiness that saps my energy. Let laughter, dance, and song be my path to balance and peace.

REACHING OUT TO OTHERS

Opening: Loving Companion, I can no longer remain separate. I want to love again. Knowing that you will not abandon me reinforces my desire to love. I trust you to sustain me as I try to reach out. Fill me with the energy of hope.

Psalm

O sing a new song;
play skillfully and loudly so all may hear.
For the word of the Creator is faithful,
and all God's works are to be trusted.
The Creator loves justice and right
and fills the earth with faithful love.

(Psalm 33:3–5)

Reflection

Healing grief has the power to enlarge our capacity to empathize with the suffering of others. Confronting our own loneliness, sorrow, and suffering invites us to care for other people, people like us.

When we grieve and let go, loss can make us better people. In the final stage of grief, the desire for loving relationships makes a tentative return once again. We might find ourselves more vulnerable to love and willing to risk loving.

If grief deepens our faith, hope, and willingness to love, then death and loss, small or great, cannot win.

Hymn

Love is as powerful as death. . . .
Love's lightning blazes with fire,
the very fire of God.
No torrent can drown the fires of love.
          (Adapted from Song of Songs 8:6–7)

Closing: Loving Companion, give me the strength to comfort others, as you have comforted me. Let me weep with those who weep and share the anguish and pain of those who you call me to help. Let me be a sign of your love. Move me to love again.

Pilgrim Ways

Opening: God, my guide, as a pilgrim I feel far from home and yearn to be delivered once and for all from isolation, loss, and suffering. Light my way, and let me rest in a place of peace. You once promised: "I shall bring you back to the place from which I exiled you" (adapted from Jeremiah 29:14). Grief has been exile. Lead me home.

Psalm

Happy those whose strength is in you;
they have courage to make the pilgrimage!
As they go through the Valley of the Weeper,
they make it a place of springs,
clothed in generous growth by early rains.
For you, God, are a sun and shield,
bestowing grace and glory.

(Psalm 84:5–6,11)

Reflection

Grief intensifies the awareness of ourselves as pilgrims who will never fully reach our goal of union with others and God in this life. We are exiles, searching for home.

God, however, welcomes those who are pilgrims and brings hope to all those who have discovered that they are homeless. God is present not only at the end of the journey, but all along the way. Even as we travel toward God, our divine guide journeys with us, a bright star directing us through dark nights.

If we listen and attend to the love and hope that we offer each other, we will experience God's intimacy and support.

Hymn

Through many dangers, toils, and snares
I have already come;
It's grace that brought me safe thus far,
and grace will lead me home.

How sweet the name of Jesus sounds
to a true believer's ear.
It soothes his sorrows and heals his wounds,
and drives away his tears.

(John Newton, "Amazing Grace")

Closing: God, my guide, take my hand and lead me along through my suffering to your love and justice, peace and freedom. May I sing and dance, joyful in your embrace.

AFTERWORD

For everything there is a season, and a time for
every matter under heaven:

    a time to be born, and a time to die;
    a time to plant, and a time to pluck up what
      is planted;

    .   .   .   .

    a time to weep, and a time to laugh;
    a time to mourn, and a time to dance;

    .   .   .   .

    a time to seek, and a time to lose;
    a time to keep, and a time to throw away;
    a time to tear, and a time to sew.
    [God] has made everything suitable for its
      time.

(Ecclesiastes 3:1–7,11)

"*Cries of the Heart* is an invaluable resource when confronted with festering wounds unresponsive to medicine. Simsic stares at grief, weeps, and with tender compassion, walks with the reader each step of the way to wholeness. He does not offer an escape, but a letting go, because only in beholding God in the darkness can one be restored to new life. This book is a cradle, an anchor, and a secure lifeline amidst the raging fury of unspeakable grief." **Isabel Guadiz, MD,** pediatrician, Fairview Park, Ohio

"When someone is suffering in grief, it is difficult to find words that are an adequate expression of one's own experience. Wayne Simsic has captured the pain of grief and transformed it into compassionate words. As I read the selections, I felt my own heart speaking. These prayers will help mourners to feel connected to God and grounded as individuals. It has value across all denominations of mourners. I find the selections helpful in my own work with the bereaved." **Savine Gross Weizman, PhD,** psychologist, bereavement therapist, senior author of *About Mourning: Support and Guidance for the Bereaved*, Beachwood, Ohio

"This book holds much comfort for the bereaved in acknowledging their loss and the ebb and flow of their grief. The content allows you to draw upon the depth of your spirit for strength and hope. For the helping professional this is an excellent resource for use at support groups and memorial services." **Carol A. Patacca, LISW,** director of bereavement and special services, Hospice Program, Cleveland, Ohio